REAL SIBLINGS

Sydney Jones

ISBN 978-1-63814-331-4 (Paperback)
ISBN 978-1-63814-332-1 (Digital)

Covenant Books, Inc.
11661 Hwy 707
Murrells Inlet, SC 29576
www.covenantbooks.com

To my sweet Kylainah,

I know that mommy has asked you to sacrifice a lot for our family to be complete. I hope you always see your siblings as "real siblings" and never lose sight of the work that God has asked us to do.

I love you the most!
Mama

This is my story—
one that's often untold.
One that you usually overlook,
Unless you've been shown.

I was born first into my family,
But I was just a start.
My mommy took in lots of kids.
They grew inside her heart.

I gained a whole house of siblings
Very, very fast.
I let myself get attached,
Hoping the love would last.

We played all day, every day;
I almost always shared my toys.
We did as Mommy told us—
We were good girls and boys.

I'll always remember them feeding me.
I love mac and cheese.
They're wrapped around my finger.
All I have to say is "Please."

Loving them is easy.
I do it every day.
Losing them is the hard part.
I always hope they stay.

There were some days I got in the car
And asked Mommy for my brother.
She would look at me with tears
And say, "He went back to his mother."

I would be sad for a day or two—
Sometimes just confused.
I knew it would get easier
Because real siblings you never lose.

My mother told me they loved me;
I believe everything she says.
"They passed through to bless our home,
As He becomes more, we become less."

Our family quotes the Bible
And Mom says that's why we are resilient.
God has a plan for our family—
We must listen to fulfill it.

For now, I know I'm staying,
Although sometimes I do consider:
"Do I have another mommy?"
"I gave birth to you," she'll whisper.

Foster? Biological? Adoptive?
I often hear these words.
"Nope, real," I tell them,
"And the other ones really hurt."

Where we grew is not so relevant
Because where we are now is what matters.
Real siblings share the same love.
We climb the same ladders.

That's right—one step at a time—
Mistakes and accomplishments too.
We will hold hands and rise
Because real siblings always do.

ABOUT THE AUTHOR

Sydney Jones is a first-time author who resides in Bowling Green, Kentucky. Sydney graduated from Western Kentucky University and now works as a licensed clinical social worker, following years of working in the foster care system. Sydney is a foster parent and mother of many: one from her womb, the others from her heart. Her love for her children inspired this story, and she hopes to show you another perspective of fostering.

CPSIA information can be obtained
at www.ICGtesting.com
Printed in the USA
JSHW012029220222
23242JS00001B/2

9 781638 143314